Living *with the* Seasons

Living *with the* Seasons

Creating a Natural Home

BY BONNIE TRUST DAHAN

PHOTOGRAPHS BY SHAUN SULLIVAN

STYLING BY ANTHONY ALBERTUS

CHRONICLE BOOKS

SAN FRANCISCO

Library of Congress Cataloging-in-Publication Data:
Dahan, Bonnie Trust.
Living with the seasons : creating a natural home / by Bonnie Trust Dahan ; photographs by Shaun Sullivan.
    p. cm.
ISBN 0-8118-3248-1
1. Interior decoration—Psychological aspects. 2. Seasons.
I. Sullivan, Shaun. II. Title.
    NK2113 .D34 2003
    747—dc21

                    2002154403

Manufactured in China

Designed by Sandra McHenry Design
Photographs by Shaun Sullivan
Styling by Anthony Albertus

Distributed in Canada by Raincoast Books
9050 Shaughnessy Street
Vancouver, British Columbia V6P 6E5

10 9 8 7 6 5 4 3 2 1

Chronicle Books LLC
85 Second Street
San Francisco, California 94105
www.chroniclebooks.com

Dedication:

To the dear friends and family whose love saw me through all the seasons of creating this book.

Acknowledgments

As always, my profound thanks and appreciation must first go to the original *Garden House* team, who helped create this latest book. Shaun Sullivan's artistry and unwillingness to compromise the potential of any image is evident in every photograph in this book. Anthony Albertus's styling brilliance, creativity, and ability to read my mind continue to amaze me even after all the years we've worked together. Sandra McHenry's design created the striking and flexible foundation that allowed us the freedom to play in every location and the structure to make the book cohesive. Leslie Jonath at Chronicle Books is the dream editor who encourages me from the sidelines, never intrudes in the creative process unnecessarily, but is there when needed. Without the gracious hospitality of numerous homeowners who opened their homes to us, *Living with the Seasons* would not exist:

George Beier and John Caner

The Butti Family

Linda and Kit Hinrichs

Gerald Reis and Kurt Fleichtmeyer

Linda Regan

Delwin Rimbey, Carl Croft, and Steve Fletcher

John Staub

Gloria, Shaun, Isabella, and Emily Sullivan

Barbara Witt

spring summer

renewal

*Spring is the palate-cleanser
season—the champagne sorbet
between courses in nature's
sumptuous meal. Spring's
hopeful signals beckon us to
unlock the creaky doors of
our imagination and integrate
seasonal design elements that
nurture a mood of promise.*

abundance

*Summer is the season of
abundance, as nature's
cornucopia of fruits and
flowers spills forth joyously.
Time itself seems more
languorous and life moves
outdoors where informality
is the order of the day.*

Introduction

This book began with the simple act of noticing.

When I moved from a home with a grand perennial, herb, and rose garden to a smaller, simpler space, I felt compelled to transplant a living symbol of the past ten years in my new home. My favorite herb, lemon verbena, planted the previous spring and flourishing that summer, seemed the right choice. Repotted in early autumn, it fared well at first. But by late in the season, it had begun dropping leaves, and come winter, it was completely barren. Even though I knew it was deciduous, I moved it to the plant graveyard behind the house, thinking that the change from ground to container must have been too much of a shock for it. Much to my delight, though, in early spring, I noticed a few tiny leaves on the deadened branches. I moved it back to its place of honor just outside the kitchen door, and the plant thrived. Its vibrant green leaves became refreshing infusions and salad ingredients

once again. ❧ As a result of these seasonal observations, I learned to love the plant's dormant branches as much as its productive green masses of leaves. In winter, the branches hold the promise and dreams of hot summer afternoons when I'll pluck a handful of leaves for a cool lemonade or salad garnish. From the life cycle of a single plant, I realized that for me, the truest beauty of all is found in the natural world, in all its moods, as it moves through the seasons. There is a particular poignancy in a knob that becomes a bud that becomes a blossom; it's still evident as the bloom turns brown, dries out, and scatters to the ground. This beauty can translate directly

to our own lives, and to our homes, if only we remember to connect with it. ❧ When nature's resources are cherished and its eloquence is embodied in a home through color, texture, fabrics, and furnishings, strict decorating rules or prescriptive room arrangements can be abandoned. Instinct takes over, and a simple glance

Summer afternoon—
summer afternoon; to
me those have always been
the two most beautiful
words in the
English language.
~Henry James

*Autumn is a second spring
when every leaf is a flower.*
~Albert Camus

outdoors provides inspiration from nature's subtle grace, extraordinary palette, range of resources, and abundance of ingredients, that are available to anyone. ❧ In the pages that follow we look at the year's cycle and its direct influence on various rooms in the home. Each season offers fresh ways to update and to enliven your surroundings

while living more in harmony with the cycles of nature. During winter's chill, we gather by the fire in the living room and dine on lavish meals. We linger in a steaming tub. We're drawn to rich, warming colors. In spring, there is an impulse to eliminate excess and begin afresh. We cast a critical eye on our bedrooms and tend toward crisper, lighter colors and textiles throughout the house. Come summer, we throw open the windows and doors to embrace the garden, which itself becomes another living space. The differentiation between indoors and out blurs, and vivid color reflects our lighter spirits. The beginning of autumn, with its cooler air and shorter days, beckons us back inside to once again begin the process of preparing the home for winter. One more burst of bright color from the last harvest, and then earthy tones come into play through tableware. In winter, we hibernate and take comfort in deep reds, greens, and pure white. A cozy throw and a cup of steaming tea turn gazing at the snowscape outside into a meditation. At any time of year, when we choose to live in harmony with the ebb and flow of the seasons, as our ancestors did by necessity, we connect with the elusive and ever-changing elements that surround us. ❧ This book is meant to gently point the way to a reunion with the natural world. You'll find ways to draw inspiration from every season and incorporate each

one into your home. Easy decorating changes or accents based on seasonal colors bring freshness and become restoratives to your home year round. In the end, living in tune with the unassuming, organic elegance of the seasons will help you to create a haven that comforts and nurtures you from the inside out. ❄

In winter we lead a more inward life. Our hearts are warm and cheery, like cottages under drifts, whose windows and doors are half concealed, but from whose chimneys the smoke cheerfully ascends.
~ Henry David Thoreau

spring

is the palate-cleanser season—the champagne sorbet between courses in nature's sumptuous meal. You don't need a calendar to know when it is early spring. You need only note the gradual lengthening of daylight, catch a whiff of warm air, and spot the first shoots of green poking up through the barren ground. As springtime unfolds, it is mirrored by your own inner awakening. Your focus shifts outward. Like a young plant stretching toward the sun, you emerge from winter's darkness, and the cycle of renewal begins once again. ❧ This is a time of year when we long to scour and scrub away any lingering winter mustiness. No wonder it's traditionally the season to clean the house from top to bottom, banishing cobwebs, dust bunnies, and smudges on the windowpanes as clear light streams in. Along with the dirt, we're moved to eliminate clutter. Tidiness, order, and simplicity drive decisions about what to keep and what to discard. Possessions that seemed relevant even a few months ago now appear superfluous. Storm windows are stowed away, and screens take their place so that we can drink in fresh air. Also ready for storage are woolen sweaters and the cashmere throw that warmed us by the fire. Nature may have some fun by mischievously teasing us with a few frosty days and plummeting

A seedling poking up from its rolled newspaper pot and the pink bloom of a striking magnolia blossom are symbols of the awakening and new growth that spring embodies. It follows that we want our home decor to be refreshed as well.

temperatures, but we're not fooled. We search the closet shelves for muted linen or cotton bedclothes that were folded and stowed last autumn. Lightweight open-weave tablecloths or bamboo place mats replace heavy jacquard as more formal tableware and place settings are exchanged for the casual. The winter pantry, filled with hot chocolate and mulling spices, holds less interest than spring onions, fresh greens, and asparagus— all suddenly available at the recently reopened farmers' market. Refreshing, spirit-lifting showers with zesty, citrusy soaps become more alluring than long soaks in the tub.

∾ Spring is a seasonal palette cleanser as well. The deep colors of autumn and winter now appear oppressively weighty. Inspiration comes instead from the subtle pastels of new life in the garden—an arrangement of greens and pale pink and white tulips or lilies. Cut to enjoy indoors at close range, these early blooms are reminders of the vivacious beauty still to come. Inspired by spring's watercolor landscape, we flirt with the possibility of transforming what now strikes us as a drab bedroom wall into a field of lavender. When we pull up a rug to expose bare floor in the living room, the results embolden us to eliminate the drapes. Basking in brighter light, the geometry of square windowpanes in late spring softens against the first bloom of the rosebush just outside. Spring's hopeful signals beckon us to unlock the creaky doors of our imagination and integrate seasonal design elements that nurture a mood of promise. ∾

The elements of this corner setting epitomize the natural home. Reclaimed Douglas fir is the wood used for these handcrafted futons. The coffee table has a bamboo top and reclaimed fir legs. Easy-to-change slipcovers and throw pillows mimic spring's subtle shades and can be updated to reflect each new season's palette. (For the same room in autumn, see page 74.)

A trip to the first farmers' market of the
year yields vivid color and an appetizing
bounty. Asparagus and yellow iris, early
harbingers of spring, revitalize a kitchen
counter and pair compatibly as table decor
for a casual lunch. The textured, architectural stalks of asparagus form a stately
miniature forest in a tumbler of water as
they await sautéing. Their short growing
season heightens the appreciation of their
delicate flavor. Natural-fiber baskets and
light wood tableware and salad bowls,
retrieved from winter storage, are the
utensils and serving pieces of choice to
complement this lush array of greens
and yellows.

This home flaunts the stunning structural angles and composition of its contemporary architecture. Poised in front of open atrium doors, the elements on the buffet table juxtapose textures and shapes that symbolize the rebirth evident everywhere outdoors. Elongated, pilsner-shape vases appear to reach toward the soaring ceiling. Dramatically filled with arching sprays of pink peonies and white tulips, they marry comfortably with the modern design while adding a much needed softening touch. Just outside the sliding doors to the atrium, shafts of sunlight nurture pink pelargonium in oversized planters. Pool moss is mounded and set on a glass plate. Araucana eggs, icons of spring's fertility, fill two hand-painted bowls and scatter on the table beneath the moss. A butter-colored raw silk table runner reflects the open weave and natural wood of a pair of armchairs.

Spring is a time to air out the bedroom and replace heavy winter quilts with light-weight bedding. In spring we become more casual in our dress and habits, and this freedom allows for simpler fabrics in the bedroom as well. Linen is a good option, with an elegant, tight weave and a cool feel against the skin. Ignore its reputation for wrinkling and allow that characteristic to become an advantage. Here sheets in pale blue are juxtaposed with transitional charcoal and taupe, which can be replaced with crisp white in the summer. Inventive storage solutions for winter bedclothes can become part of the bedroom's furnishings as well as practical space savers. The hand-woven checkerboard rug from Nepal in lighter colors replaces a more intricate and dark-toned Turkish kilim. Spotting a sapphire delphinium during a garden walk may have inspired the burst of color that three tiny vases bring to this serene scene.

25

Scandinavians have much to teach us about the art of the sauna and its powers of renewal. Spring is the ideal time to consider a sauna bath as a practical addition to the home. This one is in a small building adjacent to an outdoor shower and swimming pool. But long before the pool opens for the summer, regular saunas will help cleanse the pores and lighten the spirit. Just as our appetites in spring instinctually lead us to less heavy foods, the sauna can become a ritual "bath" that rids us of winter's rich indulgences. Like any other room in the seasonal home, this one deserves a touch of appropriate color and decor. The pattern from a solar eclipse is multiplied through the branches of a tree and projected on a nearby wall. The garden's yield of early sweet peas is displayed in a softly contoured blue pitcher set atop a tree-trunk pedestal. Inside, an oncidium orchid branch is available for contemplation.

Unlike winter, when we shake off the chill with long soaks in a hot bath, spring invites us to take a bracing shower that refreshes and enlivens us. This outdoor shower has been designed to accommodate two. Its open, airy construction allows the breeze to waft through while offering protection from an unexpected sprinkle of spring rain. Even a utilitarian outdoor room like this one can be thoughtfully appointed and changed seasonally. In spring, a buttercup-yellow folding chair punctuates the gray shingle and concrete construction. A carved Balinese wood panel lends an unexpected, exotic touch. Lightweight towels in ice blue, white, and sage green will air-dry quickly. A feathery bunch of spring forget-me-nots just collected from the garden adds a perky accent in a white enamel pitcher. Even the soaps have been chosen for the fresh citrus fragrance they impart.

Even before it's possible to step out and enjoy the first days of spring blooms in the backyard, an indoor garden can be created with a little ingenuity and playfulness. A trip to the local nursery yields potted bacopa, diascia, moss ferns, artemisia, and boxwood. Tucked into an antique child's wagon, they become an instant rolling garden and conversation piece in this light-filled sunroom. White hydrangeas displayed in an old triangular flower pot, grass in a metal plant tray, and bright yellow forced tulips add to the lighthearted sensibility. Ticking stripe fabric on the cushions combined with soft green pillows and a throw reinforce the uplifting feeling of promise and fresh growth embodied by spring.

By late spring, the garden is awash with pastel pinks, lavenders, yellows, and peaches. Taking cues from Monet's Giverny, this watercolor palette inspires outdoor seating choices that blend with the surrounding garden. Teak that has aged to a silvery gray is unobtrusive and restful, and the stone chosen for the raised perennial beds creates a textured effect. The classic American Adirondack chair and bench are placed at vantage points allowing the garden to be enjoyed to its fullest and dreams of the coming summer to be indulged.

Viewing one flower at a time in the garden calls to mind the difference between a landscape painting and a portrait. A landscape conveys garden topography, while an individual flower seen close up allows you to peer directly into the intricacy of the botanical world within its petals. To cut or not to cut, that is the only question. The exuberant delight of a lush garden can be doubled when bouquets are cut as a gift for a friend or for yourself. There are no rules when it comes to containers, as the flowers are clearly the main attraction. Reusing bottles and jars as vases can be an effective and economical way to create dramatic arrangements that showcase the singularity of each flower. They also invite a face-to-face sniff, which brings the essence of the season right to the fore. Every room, hallway, or entrance benefits from the restorative powers of a spray from the garden.

35

SCENTS
of the Seasons

Smell may be the most ancient of our senses, acting on the brain's primitive limbic system. We don't rely much on smell anymore as we negotiate our way through the world, but its influence remains profound. Of all our senses, it is the one with perhaps the greatest emotional potency. A whiff of a familiar aroma can catapult us back to a long-forgotten experience, prompting vivid recall of its every detail.

Each season of the year has its own hallmark fragrances, those quintessential aromas that evoke a place, a time in our lives, or sometimes just a rush of feeling. There's nothing quite like the perfume of wisteria to make us think of spring—with its note of promise, of winter's end, of new awakenings. Its purple reminds us that the home can use refreshing with invigorating color.

Certain scents unmistakably convey summer: salty ocean spray; the smell of the grass after a sudden rain; the heady aroma of sweet peas.

They epitomize summer, when the days are long and the garden is in its full glory. Armfuls of garden roses as bouquets in simple vases in every room, and calming lavender by the bedside, become tonics for the soul as well as indoor seasonal accents.

Autumn's aromas are pungent. A spice-laden mince pie fills the house with the season's quintessential flavors, and a blazing wood fire or lighted scented candles evoke thoughts of creature comforts as our lives become more centered indoors.

Winter is a feast of aromas that evoke jovial indoor gatherings over hot chocolate. A cluster of fresh pine boughs brought indoors, clove-studded oranges, or a bath scented with eucalyptus oil, are as revitalizing to the spirit as an invigorating woodland walk on a frosty day.

s u m m e r is the season of abundance, as nature's

cornucopia of fruits and flowers spills forth joyously. The garden overflows with flow-

ers like yarrow and lavender, and with boldly flavorful vegetables. Warm nights beckon

us to fling open the windows and revel in the fragrance of roses. Time itself seems

more languorous, as extra hours of light and more leisurely schedules invite us to

stretch day into night. ❧ In summer, life moves outdoors, where informality is the

order of the day. Entertaining is likely to take the form of picnics on the grass or late-

night dinners on the patio, and no elaborate furniture is required. A picnic table

draped with a bright cloth suffices for alfresco meals. Weathered wooden chairs posi-

tioned among the flowers offer welcome spots to sip a frosty drink and get lost in a

summer novel. Should extra guests arrive, lightweight indoor furniture can provide

handy outdoor seating, especially pleasing when it's in sherbet hues of orange, lime,

and lemon. For impromptu afternoon naps, nothing could be easier than rolling out a

beach mat under the shade of a paper parasol. ❧ Inside, the mood is similarly light

and airy. Heavy drapes come down, replaced by sheer curtains that waft in the slight-

est breeze—or by no curtains at all. Gathering spots move away from the fireplace and

Yellow flowers cut from the garden rest in a cast concrete urn in a relaxed fashion that reflects summer's easy pace. The citrus fragrance of aromatherapy candles perfumes the air, and their lime and lemon colors complete this corner arrangement.

toward the windows. The dining table needs only minimal dressing when a view of the outdoors serves as the main decor. Place mats and dishes in warm yellows and purples echo nature's sunny motifs. ❧ In place of formal rugs, sisal or seagrass evoke lazy days at the beach. Dark upholstery can be livened up with a summer wardrobe of easy-care slipcovers. Not only will they freshen the room's colors, but they also can be tossed in the washing machine whenever juicy watermelon and drippy ice-cream cones necessitate cleanup. ❧ Summer accessories are spare and unfussy: a scattering of shells or starfish, a clear bowl filled with beach glass, and of course, flowers. This is not the season for carefully studied floral arrangements. Instead, a stroll through the garden might produce a handful of audacious roses or commanding stalks of foxglove that need only the simplest everyday containers to display their splendor. ❧ In the bedroom, heavy quilts are banished in favor of a cool top sheet and a silky summer-hued duvet. Bunches of lavender set nearby will release their heady aroma as they dry. If privacy is not an issue, throw back the curtains and let the first light of day awaken you naturally, as you tune in to summer's rhythms. Or engage in the ultimate mid-summer night's fantasy and sleep outdoors. A rustic tent cabin or a covered porch makes for a vacation of sorts. ❧

Coordinating bamboo and twig patterns on these crisp linens are styled after Japanese prints in fresh green. Orchid stems in a slanted recycled-glass vase and a pure white cup and plate bedside complete this summery bedroom scene.

This wash of yarrow and lavender inspires interpretation. Each season's palette, when evoked in paint colors and textiles such as pillow covers, can act as a cyclical update. All that's needed is a good look at the garden or a summer meadow for color cues, and an imagination for ways to adapt what you've seen in your home.

There is no better way to embrace summer than to build an outdoor retreat with a few indoor creature comforts. Wistful memories of lighthearted childhood summers spent camping in the woods may have inspired this adult version of a bedroom tent. Tucked among the trees, with a salvaged garden gate standing slightly ajar, this ingenuous canvas tent cabin seems more like a secret cottage. Constructed for year-round use in temperate climates, it features a lavender framed multipaned window that allows nature's light switch—moonlight and sunshine—to determine its inhabitant's sleeping and rising rhythms. Bedclothes translate the hues in an adjacent meadow into an artful textile composition. Artifacts such as an antique trunk, thermos, and bed-table arrangement harken back to a simpler era when the livin' was easy.

Emboldened by the heat of day and the humid evening air, who hasn't thought about pushing a bed outdoors on a mid-summer night? At this beach house, no compromise is needed to enjoy the elements. Just as they would indoors, high-thread-count cotton sheets, fluffy down pillows, and a silk duvet cover adorn an antique metal bed. Diaphanous organza panels hung from the veranda roof catch a seaside breeze and waft sensuously in rhythm with the ocean's waves. Beach grass gathered in a cobalt blue French flower bucket, and a collection of starfish and shells set on a folding bamboo table, create a keen sense of place and season in this dreamy setting.

Summer's heat and vibrant light inspire an experiment with vivid color on a French bistro table set amid beds of flowering perennials. It takes no more than a can of enamel paint, an unrestrained imagination, and a willing hand to add a lively splash of lipstick pink to this floral canvas. On the table, a tousled bouquet stands ready to brighten indoor rooms. This year's planting scheme is recorded in a gardener's journal. Screened hat boxes contain collections of rose petals that have been gathered to dry into a sweet-smelling potpourri. In future colder seasons, the dried blossoms will be a fragrant reminder that evokes the variations on a color theme in this outdoor haven.

Nothing expresses "Summer!" more suc-
cinctly than a picnic on the grass—even
if the grass happens to be the lawn just
beyond your own back door. Inspired by
this season's flamboyant array of colors,
it's natural to abandon indoor activities
and head outdoors with a straw hat, a
blanket, a few colorful, plump silk cushions,
a bottle of freshly made orangeade, and
a wedge of tropical fruit. Once you're
sprawled amid the lavender and poppies,
the cerulean-blue sky and vaporous clouds
will further encourage the expansive,
carefree mood that summer engenders.
The exuberant colors and elegant
furnishings transform a patch of grass
into an inviting outdoor room.

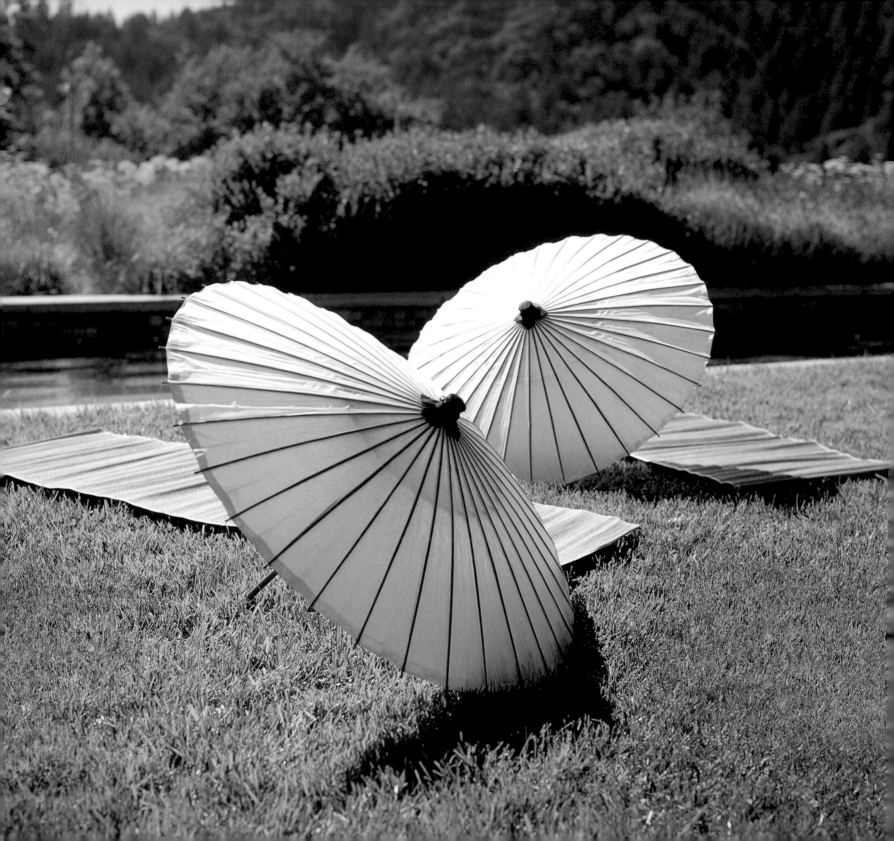

In summer, there's no need to compete with nature's opulence with expensive or high-tech outdoor furniture. Japanese parasols for shade and a tatami-inspired beach mat are all you need to create a restful outdoor space for basking in poolside pleasures. An inviting pitcher of lemonade garnished with cut lavender and lime is the recipe for a relaxing afternoon. Inhaling the clean fragrance of freshly mowed grass and enjoying a ringside view of nearby blooming lavender and yarrow after a plunge in the pool reduce this season to its profound essence.

This traditional sunken Japanese table is set for a simple lunch. Homemade egg salad and watercress on whole wheat bread, freshly brewed iced tea with lemon crescents, and a platter of cherries are the down-to-earth foods we crave at this time of year. Straightforward white tableware suggests a loose, carefree approach to the season's inclinations. A pitcher and glasses that could easily find their place on a picnic table lend a casual touch. A floral interpretation of the "ova" theme, mantilla poppies, which resemble eggs sunny side up, were pruned from a flowering bush just out the door. Paired with purple agapanthus, this bouquet is testament to the surprising marriages that can result from foraging in your own backyard.

The European custom of dining alfresco
in summertime makes great sense. Fresh
air, late-afternoon filtered lighting, and a
few rustic implements create this roman-
tic scene. Set among olive trees that
yielded a bountiful harvest, this seasonal
table celebrates the simple pleasures of
the aperitif. Without much fuss, a couple
of flea market wooden folding chairs, an
old picnic table, and a sunny tablecloth
complement a bottle of crisp white wine,
a few chunks of cheese, freshly baked
bread, and a wide array of home-cured
olives. Old but still functioning crocks
and rattan-wrapped decanters add func-
tional authenticity while a handmade
ceramic decanter also stores the oil.
A hanging lantern brings a festive note.
In other variations, this open-air dining
room could easily serve as a delightful
setting for good old-fashioned bar-
becue fare.

This clever outdoor bathing area was created from old washtubs that were converted into a double sink. They're as appropriate for fresh-air laundering as they are for washing up after a hike or an afternoon badminton tournament. An old metal pail holds biodegradable soaps and detergents. Continuing the theme, a showerhead mounted on a pole allows for quick rinses and easy drying off with towels hung within reach. A natural loofah and wooden brush in an oversized jar are set on an old metal American porch chair. Adjacent to a nearby sleeping tent, this nostalgic setup takes a back-to-basics theme and makes it an appealing option for outdoor living.

Dappled afternoon light makes icons from the 1950s look new again. Butterfly chairs sporting covers in audacious but complementary summertime hues of orange and lime find new life outdoors as lawn seating. Add a panting dog lying in the shade and two young friends who've made construction-paper pinwheels, and the quintessential lazy afternoon is complete. As evening approaches, the pinwheels will spin on puffs of air. Without much planning or effort, a family room has emerged, to be repeated next year.

The twin of this expressive arrangement
of gerbera daisies, scented geranium
leaves, and drooping green millet stems
in a weathered wooden container on the
dining room table is echoed in a nearby
wall niche. In many newer homes, one
room flows openly into the next. The
repetition of bouquets of seasonal flowers
in these light-filled living and dining rooms
serves as a visual union as the eye travels
from one space to the other. Two story
windows merge the outdoors and indoors
creating a doubled sense of space and an
abundance of natural light.

Nature's transition from one season to the next can be subtle, leaving room to blend them in your home. This table features an unconventional grouping. Rich purples of late-summer plums are juxtaposed with the chartreuse of early-autumn pears. Rather than abandon the lime-colored bowls, lavender plates, and citrus linens of previous seasons, you can integrate them as here with deeper violet chargers accented by persimmon votive candles, which herald the autumnal range of colors that lie ahead.

LIVING
Color

As each season slowly flows into the next, nature's palette shifts, like a slight turn of a kaleidoscope, bringing new colors into play and intermingling them with some from the previous season. Tuning into the landscape's revised hues and incorporating them into our interiors helps us harmonize with this natural cycle.

At times, a season's colors speak to us so strongly that we want to immerse ourselves in them, perhaps going so far as to repaint the walls or buy a new piece of furniture. More often, though, small changes can go a long way toward reviving a home and making it seasonally appropriate.

In spring, the season of rebirth, it's not surprising that we gravitate toward pastels: soft, gentle shades of yellow, blue, green, peach, lilac, pink. Spring's colors are youthful, like the pink blush of camellia blossoms or the fresh green of grass.

If spring is a whisper, then summer is a shout. It reverberates with ostentatious colors from the garden such as the riotous reds, magentas, royal blues, oranges, and yellows that playfully mix in an abundant cottage garden. You can indulge your impulses with bold primary colors and allow your imagination to run wild with unexpected combinations.

Autumn's paint box becomes more subdued and earthy, as deeply burnished hues bring welcome change from summer's brash colors. Turning leaves, shorter days, and cooler air inform us that nature's last burst of growth will soon be exhausted. Cinnamon, pumpkin, beet red, and dusky purple bring us back to our roots.

In winter we crave cozy, nurturing colors—deep red, dark green, and rich brown, to warm up our surroundings, especially in the living and dining room, where we gather with friends.

a u t u m n

is synonymous with the harvest—the season for reaping the benefits of the year's planning and work, feasting together on the bounty, and preparing for the darkening days ahead. Even those who no longer toil in the fields take pleasure in having symbols of the harvest indoors. Gourds in rich hues, shafts of wheat, a spray of autumn leaves, or a bowl of crisp apples serve as reminders of the harvest, telling us that nature is slowing down for a period of rest.

Nature's pendulum continues its slow glide toward ever shorter days and lengthening nights, reaching the cusp and crossing over at the start of autumn. Now darkness exceeds daylight. The pleasures of summer still linger, though, with an occasional glorious warm day that summons us outside and delays the inevitable migration indoors. But the crispness in the air, the magical cast of the afternoon light, and the crunch of leaves underfoot are unmistakable signs that the earth has advanced in its orbit. As the sun sets, evening's chill sends us indoors to cozy up by the fire.

Candlelight and firelight recall the once-ritual bonfire that celebrated the harvest and inspired courage against the demons of darkness. In times past, the ashes were scattered on fallow fields to nourish them. Such seasonal rituals as cleaning the chimney

The sight of red-tinged green apples on the branch and the crunch of fallen leaves underfoot encourage us to surround ourselves with warm, autumnal colors and textures as we migrate indoors.

69

and stockpiling firewood anticipate the hearth's being pressed into service once again. In autumn, our thoughts might also turn toward repairing the roof or mending a drafty window as we sense the need to batten down the hatches for the coming winter.

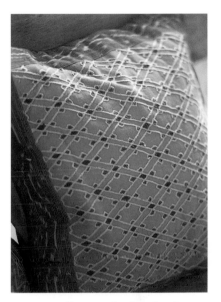

A collection of embroidered pillows in autumn colors act as a softening feature to this rustic teak settee. Set atop an old crate mounted on wheels and used as a side table, a white pumpkin signals the arrival of autumn.

With sunlight now less direct and more diffuse, summer's exuberant colors give way to a more subdued palette. We gravitate toward gold, sienna, terra cotta, and persimmon. Fabrics with a silky texture and a bit of sheen reflect firelight and warm up our rooms. Throws and shawls come out of the cedar chest to drape on sofas and chairs, ready to bring comfort from unexpected chills. Golden chrysanthemums and fiery foliage can be brought indoors as seasonal reminders of the garden in its last hurrah of the year. Just as the landscape rests under a blanket of leaves, we too seek spaces where we can nestle in as the days grow shorter. Uncluttered rooms with a few favorite objects serve as nurturing retreats, whether we enjoy them in solitude or with others. A meditative statue, a warm blanket to snuggle beneath, all refresh the spirit. We pull furniture up close to the fire as indoor pursuits occupy more and more of our time. As the spirit of autumn reaches its zenith, we celebrate the fullness of the season and the incomparable sanctuary of home.

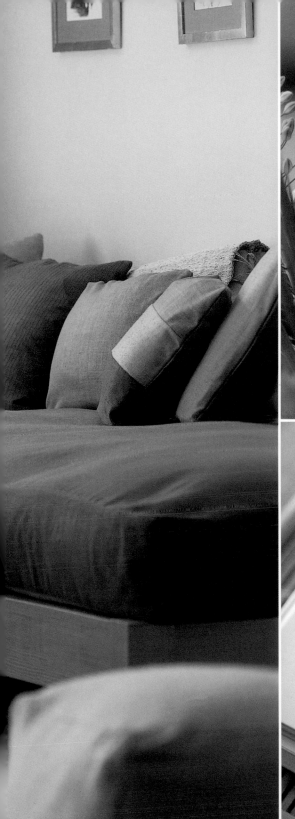

This multipurpose corner niche is the essence of seasonal living. It's not difficult to make over any space by replacing the textile accents with a color range that more accurately reflects the changes in nature. With leaves ablaze in a riot of color outside, pomegranate slipcovers on these futon mattresses replace the lighter colors used in spring and summer. (For the spring version of this room, see page 14). An array of raw silk pillow covers coordinates and introduces mustard and brown hues. A copper vase is filled with a spiky bouquet of dracaena and eremurus flowers. A textured pod makes its elegant statement on a stack of books set in a bamboo tray. Even the botanical prints on the walls can be changed each autumn to reflect outdoor plant life.

This designer's workspace has been edited down to a minimalist perspective of well-chosen seasonal symbols. As the changing weather naturally encourages us to turn inward, a studio like this becomes an ideal environment for autumnal contemplation. Burnt sienna walls dramatically accented by black door frames provide a fresh and sophisticated look. Rolls of drawings and sketches are functionally stored in a large glass vase and add architectural elegance. Gourds placed within and perched on glass cylinders are elevated to become seasonal sculptures and extend the squash family theme. A speckled swan-necked gourd lounges in a rope-tied harvest basket. Fern fronds posed gracefully in a carved mango-wood vase soften the high contrast of color with unexpected brush strokes of vivid green.

The utter simplicity of a sheaf of wheat
wrapped in linen and placed carefully on
a low table is an icon that indicates the
approaching autumn. Layered bedclothes
in rust, amber, and mocha transform the
oversized bamboo bed into a restful
refuge. Silk pillows are set against a
block-printed jute coverlet. A cup of
chamomile tea is set on a bed tray to
invite a late afternoon nap. Candlelight is
equally appropriate in the bedroom, as in
other rooms in this season. A zinc vase
on a bedside table holding a simple spray
of dark-pink lilies offers punctuation. The
same lilies are used in a double-tiered
Japanese vase that decorates the top of
the tansu chest.

As the days shorten, there is an inclina-
tion to linger as long as possible outdoors to capture the last moments of
autumn. An outdoor fireplace and a ram-
bling porch invite a twilight gathering.
Screened lanterns prevent the candle
flames from being extinguished if an
evening breeze picks up. A bundle of
lavender branches tossed into the fire
mingles an aromatic vestige of summer
with the wood smoke. Rustic wooden
furniture, left outdoors year round, has
by now aged to muted tones of gray.
Vibrant autumn colors flame-stitched on
Indian throw pillows—pomegranate reds,
persimmon orange, maple leaf magenta—
pick up on the fireplace theme. Pumpkins
of every hue, from creamy white to pale
green to gold, line the shelves next to
the fireplace and pose as still lifes on the
tables. An old-fashioned popcorn popper
has been called into service for an all-
time favorite snack.

This setting of rich wood furnishings juxta-posed with bright plants artfully blends warmth with a confident sense of color. The water hyacinth dining chairs offer textural relief and play nicely against the deep brown wood of the sideboard and dining table. Seasonal touches of red are brought into play with the napkins and the boxes used as pedestals. Red oncidium orchid sprays pick up on the theme and play off the red centers of lime-green cymbidium orchid branches. Rows of votive candles in chunky glass cups set on copper trays bring a warm and subtle glow. The florals help coordinate with the chartreuse wall color, a reminder of summer exuberance.

83

A sleek tropical wood lounge is positioned
near a huge multipaned window to best
enjoy the late-afternoon light of autumn.
The defiantly bold striped cover and
pillows on the window seat play off a
cluster of orange persimmons. In another
part of the room, seating by a rammed-
earth fireplace features layers of natural
textures: a rattan porch chair, a hemp
rug, and a stack of seagrass cushions.
A composition of brightly colored glass-
ware atop the mantel reflects the light
and coordinates with the textiles.

Even with the predominantly Asian decor in this multipurpose room, bright spots of autumn color seem completely appropriate. On a stone table behind the daybed, an artful arrangement of yellow chrysanthemum and vivid orange lilies is juxtaposed against a large vase displaying simple branches. An L-shaped metal container with six bamboo tubes holds local grasses and tiny yellow chrysanthemums. A meditation area in spring, an extra guest room in autumn, and a den or living room in winter are all possible interpretations of this one balanced and serene space.

A teak library bench softened with dark throw pillows extends the seating space in this indoor/outdoor room. The floor-to-ceiling windows unite the continually changing seasonal views outside with the indoor space. A playful set of leaf stamps is a cue to the time of year, as are the pomegranate-paste delicacies. It's important to remember that the view into the room from outside is just as important as the experience you have within it.

An attic or loft space that seems big enough only for storage can be reenvisioned as a cozy autumn "nest." After all, heat does rise, and warmth is what we seek during chillier months. It doesn't take much to create an extra sleeping space for guests or a snug perch for young yearlong residents. Absolutely required are piles of downy pillows, fluffy comforters, and warm blankets, as well as a rug and an extra throw. A wooden tray set on an antique Asian rice basket improvised as a bedside table holds a steaming pot of hot cider at the ready. Somehow, having to climb up to a hidden haven in the rafters enhances the experience of this intimate spot.

SEASONAL
Textures

Even the most comfortable furniture and pleasing color palette can still yield a room that feels a bit flat and uninviting if the overall scheme lacks textural variety. All the myriad details in a room contribute texture: furniture, fabrics, plants, rugs, tableware, accessories. Mixing those textures to create a balance of smooth and rough, shiny and matte, wood and upholstery provides the pop that makes a space come alive.

Depending on where they're used, textures may be experienced tactilely or purely visually. Plush velvet upholstery, bamboo place mats, linen sheets, and Egyptian cotton towels are all enjoyed through direct contact with our skin. A shiny copper vase, clear jars stuffed with grains, a stack of river stones, or filmy curtains that diffuse the sunlight give us pleasure simply by looking at them.

Being sensitive to the unique feel of each season allows us to edit a room's materials to harmonize with nature. In the warmer months

we favor lighter textures. Crisp cotton and linen, grass sprouting in a pot, or a bowl of delicately hued eggshells suits the mood of spring's revival. In summer, silky fabrics feel best, bright flowers from the garden lend a splash of freshness, and the fewer objects overall, the better.

Colder months call for richer textures and more layers, not just for the physical warmth they provide but also because of their satisfying visual weight. An extra chenille or cashmere throw on the couch is comforting on a chilly night. A bed dressed in flannel sheets and piled with comforters lures us to sleep early. Shiny copper buckets, rough-hewn baskets stacked with wood, or a collection of pinecones adds welcome heft to a room's appearance.

Just as cooking with what's in season brings us in synch with our local climate, relying on seasonal materials to populate the home provides nourishment for the soul.

w i n t e r is often a time of contradictory impulses.

Modern culture sets a frantic pace filled with family-reunion excursions, gift-buying

sprees, and social events that encourage us to be seen and heard at the top of our

game. We're on, but not always by choice at a time of year when our instincts tell us

to slow down, snuggle up with a good book, or contemplate the quiet beauty of a

snow-blanketed landscape from a cozy vantage point. Bringing that seasonal need

for reflection inside means creating restful spaces. You might consider transforming

a library corner into an adult nap room, converting an attic space into a snug guest

room for unexpected company, or adding decorative accents that honor winter's spare

beauty. Throws and shawls kept close at hand throughout your house or apartment

offer comfort, warmth, and contentment. ❄ In winter, too, bed becomes more

than a place to sleep; it can be a cocoon where we nestle in and avoid blustery storms,

biting winds, and snow gusts, especially when books, extra blankets, glowing lamps,

and a pot of tea are within easy reach. Even in the living room, a couch is a welcome

retreat for daydreaming. Accessories that might have felt oppressive in the heat of

summer now seem nurturing. Extra pillows, rugs underfoot, draperies to shut out the

Forcing bulbs like narcissus, amaryllis, and hyacinth in winter, while it storms out-side, can satisfy the yearning to garden year-round.

95

darkness and cold—this layering on of textiles in warm colors and cosseting textures provides solace. ❄ The idea of taking refuge in the warmth and comfort of home has been with us for so long that by now it must be an element of our collective gene pool. In winter, a hot bath becomes a retreat, as well as an inducement to relax. A fireplace takes its rightful historical position as the central gathering spot around which stories are told, philosophy and politics are debated, and emotional warmth mingles with heat from the hearth. Above it sits a mantel that awaits your personal touch. You might choose to create an understated collage with easily gathered boughs and branches and pinecones, or other natural gleanings that reflect the colors and moods of winter. Bright red pyracantha or holly berries show off the season's favorite accent color. In the wild, such crimson delicacies are a beacon in the spare landscape, attracting birds to feast and scatter seeds for future growth. Crimson-berried branches can fill vases throughout the house, where they might be allowed to dry until season's end. Clustered in a wreath, they pay homage to a time-honored symbol of winter—a ring of living material symbolizing nature's continuity and renewal. ❄

Dishes and vases remain constant, but a runner in wintry reds and greens changes the seasonal feeling evoked in this dining room. Snipped branches of berries and crimson rose petals strewn on the table provide botanical updates. The same recycled-glass plate makes the perfect platform for a star-shaped candle. (For a spring version of this table setting, see page 22.)

darkness and cold—this layering on of textiles in warm colors and cosseting textures provides solace. ❋ The idea of taking refuge in the warmth and comfort of home has been with us for so long that by now it must be an element of our collective gene pool. In winter, a hot bath becomes a retreat, as well as an inducement to relax. A fireplace takes its rightful historical position as the central gathering spot around which stories are told, philosophy and politics are debated, and emotional warmth mingles with heat from the hearth. Above it sits a mantel that awaits your personal touch. You might choose to create an understated collage with easily gathered boughs and branches and pinecones, or other natural gleanings that reflect the colors and moods of winter. Bright red pyracantha or holly berries show off the season's favorite accent color. In the wild, such crimson delicacies are a beacon in the spare landscape, attracting birds to feast and scatter seeds for future growth. Crimson-berried branches can fill vases throughout the house, where they might be allowed to dry until season's end. Clustered in a wreath, they pay homage to a time-honored symbol of winter—a ring of living material symbolizing nature's continuity and renewal. ❋

Dishes and vases remain constant, but a runner in wintry reds and greens changes the seasonal feeling evoked in this dining room. Snipped branches of berries and crimson rose petals strewn on the table provide botanical updates. The same recycled-glass plate makes the perfect platform for a star-shaped candle. (For a spring version of this table setting, see page 22.)

w i n t e r is often a time of contradictory impulses.

Modern culture sets a frantic pace filled with family-reunion excursions, gift-buying

sprees, and social events that encourage us to be seen and heard at the top of our

game. We're on, but not always by choice at a time of year when our instincts tell us

to slow down, snuggle up with a good book, or contemplate the quiet beauty of a

snow-blanketed landscape from a cozy vantage point. Bringing that seasonal need

for reflection inside means creating restful spaces. You might consider transforming

a library corner into an adult nap room, converting an attic space into a snug guest

room for unexpected company, or adding decorative accents that honor winter's spare

Forcing bulbs like narcissus, amaryllis, and hyacinth in winter, while it storms outside, can satisfy the yearning to garden year-round.

beauty. Throws and shawls kept close at hand throughout your house or apartment

offer comfort, warmth, and contentment. ❋ In winter, too, bed becomes more

than a place to sleep; it can be a cocoon where we nestle in and avoid blustery storms,

biting winds, and snow gusts, especially when books, extra blankets, glowing lamps,

and a pot of tea are within easy reach. Even in the living room, a couch is a welcome

retreat for daydreaming. Accessories that might have felt oppressive in the heat of

summer now seem nurturing. Extra pillows, rugs underfoot, draperies to shut out the

95

SEASONAL
Textures

Even the most comfortable furniture and pleasing color palette can still yield a room that feels a bit flat and uninviting if the overall scheme lacks textural variety. All the myriad details in a room contribute texture: furniture, fabrics, plants, rugs, tableware, accessories. Mixing those textures to create a balance of smooth and rough, shiny and matte, wood and upholstery provides the pop that makes a space come alive.

Depending on where they're used, textures may be experienced tactilely or purely visually. Plush velvet upholstery, bamboo place mats, linen sheets, and Egyptian cotton towels are all enjoyed through direct contact with our skin. A shiny copper vase, clear jars stuffed with grains, a stack of river stones, or filmy curtains that diffuse the sunlight give us pleasure simply by looking at them.

Being sensitive to the unique feel of each season allows us to edit a room's materials to harmonize with nature. In the warmer months we favor lighter textures. Crisp cotton and linen, grass sprouting in a pot, or a bowl of delicately hued eggshells suits the mood of spring's revival. In summer, silky fabrics feel best, bright flowers from the garden lend a splash of freshness, and the fewer objects overall, the better.

Colder months call for richer textures and more layers, not just for the physical warmth they provide but also because of their satisfying visual weight. An extra chenille or cashmere throw on the couch is comforting on a chilly night. A bed dressed in flannel sheets and piled with comforters lures us to sleep early. Shiny copper buckets, rough-hewn baskets stacked with wood, or a collection of pinecones adds welcome heft to a room's appearance.

Just as cooking with what's in season brings us in synch with our local climate, relying on seasonal materials to populate the home provides nourishment for the soul.

92

An attic or loft space that seems big enough only for storage can be reenvisioned as a cozy autumn "nest." After all, heat does rise, and warmth is what we seek during chillier months. It doesn't take much to create an extra sleeping space for guests or a snug perch for young yearlong residents. Absolutely required are piles of downy pillows, fluffy comforters, and warm blankets, as well as a rug and an extra throw. A wooden tray set on an antique Asian rice basket improvised as a bedside table holds a steaming pot of hot cider at the ready. Somehow, having to climb up to a hidden haven in the rafters enhances the experience of this intimate spot.

A teak library bench softened with dark throw pillows extends the seating space in this indoor/outdoor room. The floor-to-ceiling windows unite the continually changing seasonal views outside with the indoor space. A playful set of leaf stamps is a cue to the time of year, as are the pomegranate-paste delicacies. It's important to remember that the view into the room from outside is just as important as the experience you have within it.

Even with the predominantly Asian decor in this multipurpose room, bright spots of autumn color seem completely appropriate. On a stone table behind the daybed, an artful arrangement of yellow chrysanthemum and vivid orange lilies is juxtaposed against a large vase displaying simple branches. An L-shaped metal container with six bamboo tubes holds local grasses and tiny yellow chrysanthemums. A meditation area in spring, an extra guest room in autumn, and a den or living room in winter are all possible interpretations of this one balanced and serene space.

Nothing embodies winter more than the fireplace. As our ancestors have done for centuries, we instinctively gather by the hearth. Yet creating an appropriate environment without replacing more casual furniture can be a challenge. Here it is achieved with color, texture, and candlelight. Rather than repainting the entire room, the red fireplace becomes a focal point that other elements can play off. A wreath on the mantel and a vase of pyracantha berries continue the crimson theme. An over-sized seagrass market basket coordinates with the chairs and becomes a fireside holder for kindling. In various tones of red, a hand-woven wool runner, a worn book, an antique brush, and a sea-glass plate also enrich the scene. Botatnical illustrations of climbing wild cucumber rolled inside antique glass jars serve as reminders of summer. Greens and pinecones are seasonal specimens that demand closer scrutiny under glass. Displayed on a large wooden tray with seedpods from salvia, wisteria pods, and lichen, the entire arrangement is proof that resourcefulness adds delight in any season.

The expected formal table settings of winter are abandoned here in favor of a more woodsy, rustic approach that marries well with these furnishings. Recently gathered pinecones and pods mingle with pomegranates and tall votive candles in juice glasses on a woven red wool runner. Even the frosted green recycled-glass goblets have an earthy silhouette. An assortment of unmatched wooden chairs and a comfortable rattan armchair further contribute to the informality. Lichen-laden branches and fir assembled in a large green glass storage jar accompany an ornate candelabra that has been converted to electric lighting. An utter lack of pretension and seasonal resourcefulness lend appealing grace to this winter dining room.

What could be cozier on a chilly winter morning than lingering in a bed dressed with flannel sheets, pillowcases, and comforter cover? Ruby-red pillows, a chenille throw, and seasonal color accents add their own warmth to this comfy nest. Gauzy fabric that changes color each season drapes over the bed from the slatted wooden wall to create an intimate, tent-like effect. This room is also a study in the calming effect of natural elements. From the rammed-earth wall to a carved tree-stump bedside table, there is a sense of deliberate connection to the outside world. Vivid green, feathery broom-plant branches in a simple glass cylinder are the only plant materials needed. A fluffy, undyed wool rug sits bedside. Stalks of bamboo that have been baked into charcoal provide an organic room freshener that purifies the air. An unused window seat in the corner of the room becomes a platform for a composition of out-of-the-ordinary cherished items and brightly colored silk boxes.

One area in the home that often reflects nature's cycles is the kitchen. One look at pantry shelves reminds us that we eat according to the weather outside. In winter, as we prepare more soups and stews, casseroles, soup pots, and large tureens are pulled forward. The spice rack is restocked with warming nutmeg, cloves, star anise, and cinnamon sticks that complement yams, squashes, and root vegetables. The electric mixer becomes a well-used tool for baking projects. Steaming bowls of thick, home-made oatmeal and rich cocoa bring their own form of soulful comfort. A delicious dessert such as poached pears fills the home with its sweet, tempting aroma. Living in tune with the seasons means cooking that way as well.

Expressing a season indoors is a form of personal taste and expression. There are no rules, and conventional solutions can be ignored or adjusted to accommodate your particular lifestyle. A minimalist approach using a simple collection of winter objects brings a contemporary setting like this in tune with the outdoors at no compromise to this very particular aesthetic.

Traditional symbols of winter take on
a completely refreshed demeanor when
posed in this contemporary setting.
Stacks of long cinnamon sticks with a
large pinecone set atop them become
a sophisticated, expressive sculpture.
Translucent green glass balls held in
a fiber nest provide a fresh, shimmering
touch. Even a collection of pinecones
looks like a new idea when it's held in
a large, low basket. Red flower buckets
and pillows look dramatic against the
black tile fireplace and armchairs. Stacks
of kiri wood boxes can hold gifts. In a
simple, understated manner they also can
be grouped together to become fitting
pedestals for pinecones and balls.

Afternoon naps and early bedtimes are part of our inward focus in winter, and our homes can accommodate these living patterns. Outfitting one side of a large living room with window-to-ceiling bookshelves turns it into a cozy den. Sliding a queen-size bed under the windowsills creates a reading and dreaming corner dedicated to respite and reflection. Neutral colors add to the serene setting. A red and green flowered pashmina shawl awaits to cosset the reader, and the iron teapots displayed above are ready for brewing hot ginger tea on a cold evening. Yarrow dried from a summer garden adds warmth with a well-preserved yellow hue. A cup of tea, a good book, and a barren meadow viewed through the window are all united in this carefully conceived, seasonally appropriate corner.

In winter, after strenuous outdoor exercise such as skiing, or merely to warm a chilled body, there is nothing more comforting than a good long soak in the tub. Often overlooked as a sanctuary for the senses, the bath is one room that has been elevated in most Japanese homes beyond mere function. The ritual of bathing is an honored part of every day that Westerners should be encouraged to explore as an antidote to stress. This bathroom has a lower faucet set into the concrete tiled wall to accommodate this perspective. Because the Japanese distinguish between washing and bathing, two bathing accessories are essential: a tiny cedar stool and a wooden bucket. Sitting on the stool, you fill the bucket and then rinse off the dirt and grime carried in from the outside. The sunken tub is then used for an initial soaking. After a few minutes soak, you give yourself a thorough scrubbing out of the tub and follow it with a final long soak. Here, the Japanese design motif extends to every detail, including the cast-iron lantern and carved wooden towel rack.

SEASONAL
Rituals

In times past, when so much of daily life revolved around growing, gathering, or catching the food that reached the table and warding off the elements, people were exquisitly attuned to the cycles of the seasons. As a result, a wealth of rituals evolved to honor nature's power.

Although these were magnificently diverse, they shared common motifs: Spring typically honors the earth's fecundity and rebirth. The Iroquois' spring thunder ceremony honored the rain that nourished the fields. Summer solstice festivals, once ubiquitous in Europe, paid homage to this season of abundance, when healing herbs were thought to be at their most potent. Harvest ceremonies—from the Jewish Sukkoth, to the lusty Greek Dionysia and Roman Bacchanalia—gave thanks for nature's offerings and helped people mentally steel themselves for the coming of darker days.

And winter—with its perils as well as its promise for rebirth to follow—led people to rallying behind the victory of light over darkness. From the Celtic day of Yule to the Norse Mother Night, countless cultures devised rituals and myths that offer hope of new life springing from old.

Today, we barely take note of the longest day or night of the year. Yet, we still respond to the ancient cycles of light and dark with more personal rituals In spring, we plant seeds, and we share the garden with butterflies and hummingbirds; summer beckons us outdoors to live every moment of prolonged daylight there. In autumn's waning daylight and chillier air, we pile kindling and logs in the fireplace and enjoy the nurturing effect of candlelight. In winter, we plant bulbs only to be delighted by their springtime blooms. Taking time to honor the year's turning points brings a sense of connection to the universe's reassuring predictability. Whether we celebrate traditional holidays or devise our own small rituals—such practices connect us to the universal thread of life.

Resource Guide

Architectural Plants
Lidsey Road Nursery
Woodgate
Chichester PS20 6SU
United Kingdom
01243 545008
Horicultural oddities and accessories.
Spend the day.

Aria
1522 Grant Avenue
San Francisco, CA 94133
415.433.0219
Obscure French and American
objects from the nineteenth
century on. Industrial lighting and
furniture oddities.

Chelsea Gardener
125 Sydney Street
London SW3
United Kingdom
0207 352 5656
Everything for the sensational garden.

Cliff's Variety
479 Castro Street
San Francisco, CA 94114
415.431.5365
Like an old five-and-dime with everything one would need to fulfill
creative endeavors.

Conran Shop
Michelin House
81 Fulham Road
London SW3
United Kingdom
020 7589 7401
and
The Terrance Conran Shop
407 E. 59th Street
New York, NY 10022
212.755.9079
Ever brilliant style in home
decor and accessories.

Crate and Barrel
800.323.5461
Stores in the U.S. nationwide
and catalog. Vases, containers,
furniture, and more with
contemporary style and diversity.

Dandelion
55 Potrero Avenue
San Francisco, CA 94103
415.436.9500
Objects for the home with a sensual,
East/West fusion. Superb zinc and
bronze vases.

Den
849 Valencia Street
San Francisco, CA 94110
415.282.6646
Twentieth-century furniture, art, and
decor with a concise, clean, modern
aesthetic.

Design within Reach
800.944.2233
Showrooms and catalog. Chic and
stylish furniture, lighting of modern
consciousness.

Eckersley Flowers
Kooyong Village
Kooyong VIC
Australia
(03) 9822 5583
Inventive arrangements and
inspirational accessories.

Flower Temple
98-100 Station Street
Fairfield, VIC
Australia
(03) 9864 9634 or 0418 134 258
Dedicated to tropical blooms and
Australian-made tableware.

The Gardener
1836 Fourth Street
Berkeley, CA 94710
510.548.4545
Soulful home accoutrements and
hand-rendered goods. For those with
appreciation for inspired objects.

Gardeners Eden
800.822.1214
Stores and catalog. Elegant
garden furniture, dinnerware,
and plants (such as miniature
growing pineapple).

Geoff Ireland
20 Lygon Street
Carlton, VIC
Australia
(03) 9347 3200
and
160 Queen St
Melbourne, VIC 3000
Australia
(03) 9602 5361
Innovative floral designs and
accessories.

George
2411 California Street
San Francisco, CA 94115
415.441.0564
and
1829 Fourth Street
Berkeley, CA 94710
510.644.1033
Where to shop for Fido and Fifi
when you won't compromise for
less than perfect pet beds, bowls, and
winter-ready weather garments.

Grey Gardens
Montauk Highway
Bridgehampton, NY 11932
631.537.4848
Antique furnishings with a clean, airy
and light palette.

Ikea
800.434.4532
Stores worldwide. Efficient,
affordable, resourceful design.
Galvanized containers, vases,
ceramic pots. Endless.

Indigo
To the trade
200 Gate Five Road, #116
Sausalito, CA 94965
415.339.9500
An eclectic assortment of elegantly
designed home furnishings from
around the world. Available in scores
of contemporary home and gift
stores nationwide.

Interieur Perdue
340 Bryant Street
San Francisco, CA 94107
415.543.1616
Rural French garden antiques and
curiosities. Furniture, ornaments,
linens, all directly imported and
brilliantly inspired.

Limn
290 Townsend Street
San Francisco, CA 94107
415.543.5466
and
501 Arden Way
Sacramento, CA 95815
916.564.2900
Exemplary selection of the best modern design. Very complete. Silverware
to sofas. Lighting to vanities.

Living Green
3 Henry Adams Street
San Francisco, CA 94103
415.864.6355
Plantscape design. Garden containers,
plants, and art pieces culled from
Asia, South America, and beyond.

Marders
Snake Hollow Road
PO Box 1261
Bridgehampton, NY 11932
631.537.3700
One of the most exceptional
nurseries. Diverse collection of trees
to interior flora and accessories.

Martha Stewart
The Catalog for Living
800.950.7130
Ready for every season, the shopper's
manual for simple, well-crafted home
supplies.

Museum of Modern Art, New York
800.447.6662
Store and catalog. From grassy
picnic mats to paper vases. Techy
and sensual, early modern and
today's modern design.

Ohmega Salvage
2407 San Pablo Avenue
Berkeley, CA 94703
510.843.7368
Top quality architectural salvage.
Knobs, windows, ironwork, and
ornament flourishes.

OK
8303 W. 3rd Street
Los Angeles, CA 90048
323.653.3501
Refined yet loose and natural accessories, art and books of the twentieth-
and twenty-first century home.

Paula Rubenstein Ltd.
65 Prince Street
New York, NY 10012
212.966.8954
Vintage quilts, quietly beautiful
antiques, ephemera.

Paxton Gate
824 Valencia Street
San Francisco, CA 94110
415.824.1872
The oddest garden store of all.
Glass orbs in astronomical colors,
tillandsias, Japanese tools, all with
an appreciation for less-obvious
natural beauty.

Pottery Barn
800.922.9934
Stores in the U.S. nationwide
and catalog nationwide. Classic
and seasonal options for the
evolving home.

Privet Cove
69 Jobs Lane
Southhampton, NY 11968
631.287.5685
Fetching collection of fresh interior
goods, old and new. Taste makers for
tasteful scouts.

Pure Seasons
800.721.3909 and
www.pureseasons.com
The season-attuned catalog and Web
site of organic, stylish, goods made
from sustainable resources. Food to
home furnishings to fashion.

Rayon Vert
3187 Sixteenth Street
San Francisco, CA 94103
415.861.3516
Vases, lighting, gorgeous flowers and
select plants.

Restoration Hardware
800.762.1005
Stores and catalog. Witty and well-
resourced home goods and furniture,
covering the whole home with style.

Smith & Hawken
800.776.3336
Stores in the U.S. nationwide
and catalog. Venerable source for
tasteful garden goods. Furniture
that lasts and looks good.

Sue Fisher King
3067 Sacramento Street
San Francisco, CA 94115
415.922.7276
Timeless style in linens. Tabletop,
personal care, and desk goods.

Z Gallerie
800.358.8288
Stores in the U.S. nationwide.
World-resourced decorative
accessories. Indian lanterns to
vases to pillows.

Zonal
1942 Fillmore Street
San Francisco, CA 94115
415.359.9111
and 4+ other Bay Area stores
Purveyor of seating, storage and
slumber oriented furnishings.
Rusty to rich.

Credits

pages 84–85, 104–105
George Beier and John Caner thank
Anni Tilt and David Arkin of
Arkin Tilt Architects
Albany, CA
and
Charles Netzow Construction
Trinidad, CA

pages, 16, 46–47, 62–65, 76–77
Interior design, Gerald Reis
Gerald Reis Design
Cloverdale, CA

pages 26–29, 44–45, 52-53, 58–71,
80–81, 90–91, 100-103, 112–113
Design, Jonathon Staub
Your Space Inc.
San Francisco, CA

pages 20–21, 54–55, 78–79, 86–89,
114–115, 117
Exterior and Interior design,
Delwin Rimbey
Tampopo
San Francisco, CA

pages 20–21, 108–111
Architect, William Leddy
Leddy Maytum Stacey Architects
San Francisco, CA